MAGNIFICENT CREATURES OF THE
Mediterranean Sea

Learn About Animals Including Sharks, Sea Urchins, Cuttlefish, and the Fried Egg Jellyfish!

Nicole K. Orr

Tidal pools on the island of Sicily fill with water at high tide. Sea anemones (uh-NEH-moh-nees), small crabs, and small fish live in these rock pools.

Welcome to the Mediterranean (**meh-dih-ter-AY-nee-an**) Sea! This sea lies between Europe (**YUR-up**) and Africa and connects to the Atlantic Ocean.

Sicily (**SIH-suh-lee**) is the largest of the Mediterranean Sea's many islands. For thousands of years, people from the rocky island of Sicily have fished the Mediterranean.

In the western part of the Mediterranean Sea lives the long-finned pilot whale. Like other small whales, pilot whales are actually a type of dolphin. Pilot whales are very social. They swim in groups of 40 to 100! Their babies, known as "calves," stay with their mothers for life.

Long-finned pilot whales are also known as "pothead whales" because their round heads look like black pots or cauldrons.

Striped dolphins swim so fast, they are sometimes called "streakers." They can swim up to 23 miles (37 kilometers) per hour!

Humans can only stay underwater for 1 to 2 minutes. Bottlenose dolphins can stay underwater for 10 to 15 minutes!

Dolphins are some of the smartest animals in the Mediterranean Sea. Bottlenose dolphins can be taught to do tricks, and they recognize themselves in mirrors. These mammals have their own language of squeaks and whistles. They've even been seen using objects as tools to reach food!

Fin whales are filter feeders. They have two large filters called baleen **(BAL-een)** that swing down from their upper jaw. The whale opens its mouth wide. Then, it pushes the water back out through the baleen. The water escapes, but not the fish that are in it. The whale then swallows the fish. Fin whales are the second-largest animal in the world, just short of the blue whale.

Fin whales are also called "razorback" whales because they have a razor-like ridge from their dorsal fin down to their tail.

A group of jellyfish is called a "smack," "bloom," or "fluther." The most common jellyfish in the Mediterranean Sea is the Mediterranean jellyfish, also known as the "fried egg jellyfish" because its bell looks a lot like an egg fried sunny-side-up!

There are many types of jellyfish found in the Mediterranean. One unusual one is the mauve (mohv) stinger. These jellyfish are transparent and have pink or purplish spots all over. They even glow in the dark! Unlike most other jellyfish, they have stinging cells on their bells as well as their tentacles.

There are 47 kinds of sharks in the Mediterranean Sea. One of the most interesting is the shortfin mako shark. These sharks are very fast and athletic, so they are popular with sport fishers. The strongest shark bite ever recorded was from a shortfin mako. The shark bit with 3,000 pounds (1,360.8 kilograms) of force.

    Another shark sharing this sea is the oceanic whitetip shark. These sharks don't have any favorite foods. They're kind of like the clean-up crew of the sea. They eat whatever leftovers are drifting around in the water.

When lots of sharks travel together, they are called a "frenzy," "gam," or "shiver." Oceanic whitetip sharks usually stay on their own, but they gather in places where they can find a lot of food.

The largest fish in the Mediterranean Sea is the basking shark. It is a type of shark that only eats plankton. They are known as "basking" sharks because they often move slowly near the ocean's surface and look like they are basking in the warmth of the sun. They can grow up to 40 feet (12.2 meters) long. That's longer than a telephone pole!

The inside of the basking shark's mouth is white. When the shark opens its huge mouth wide, large amounts of water enter and pass through the black gills, which have something called "rakers." These rakers filter out the plankton and let the water continue through. That's how the basking shark eats!

Sea urchins live along the rocky coasts of the Mediterranean Sea. These creatures look like balls covered in sharp spikes. Purple sea urchins are one of the most common types found in the Mediterranean. They eat algae and seagrass, so they prefer shallower waters and tide pools. Their spikes can be purple in color, but they can also have spikes that are brown or green.

There are over 900 kinds of sea urchins. Most live about 30 years, but some can live for over 200 years! Another common species in the Mediterranean is the black sea urchin. They cling to rocks in shallow coastal waters.

While they do not attack humans, the greater weever is one of the most venomous fish in the Mediterranean. These fish have venomous spines on their backs and venomous thorns on their gill covers. They are also unusual because they don't have a swim bladder to keep them afloat. If they stop swimming, they sink to the seafloor.

Greater weevers hunt for food by digging down into the sand. Because they're hard to see, people are sometimes injured when they accidentally step on a fish.

Tufted ghost crabs cannot swim, but if they turn upside down in the water, female ghost crabs can float. They live at the Mediterranean's edge, wetting their gills in the surf to help them breathe.

Tufted ghost crabs are the color of sand, which makes them nearly invisible as they walk across the beach.

The Mediterranean has a ton of animals that really stand out, but the cuttlefish might be the most unusual. These amazing animals have three hearts, blue blood, and even a brain that's shaped like a doughnut! Their brains might be the most impressive part—they can count, have amazing memories, and even understand waiting for rewards!

Cuttlefish have amazing eyes! Their pupils are shaped like the letter W, so they can see almost entirely behind themselves! They can also see differences in polarized light that humans can't see.

Baby turtles are called hatchlings. When hatchlings first break out of their eggs on the beach, they must use their new flippers to reach the water. Then, they swim away from the beach. This is called the frenzy period.

The loggerhead turtle is one of the world's largest turtles. What makes this turtle so exciting? It has a mouth so powerful, it can crush the shells of sea urchins and clams for food. Female loggerhead turtles have really good memories. When they are ready to have babies, they travel all the way back to where they were born. There, they dig a hole for their eggs. Their babies hatch in the same place their mothers did.

Mediterranean monk seals are the rarest species of seal in the world. There are only about 700 Mediterranean monk seals, and they all live in areas around the Mediterranean Sea. They are excellent swimmers and hunters. People have even seen them lifting rocks to hunt for prey! Their favorite foods are octopus, squid, and eels.

When they're born, Mediterranean monk seals have thick dark fur and white stripes on their bellies. In a few weeks, they lose this for adult fur. Adult Mediterranean monk seals are thought to have the shortest hair of any type of seal.

Mediterranean gulls used to be found mostly around the eastern Mediterranean Sea, but now they live all over Europe! When they are looking for mates, they grow black feathers all over their heads. Throughout the rest of the year, they have a lighter mask just around their eyes.

When they hatch, Mediterranean gulls have their eyes open and have downy gray feathers. Within 40 days, they become fledglings, growing their adult feathers and getting ready to fly.

FURTHER READING

Books

Callery, Sean. *Life Cycles: Ocean*. New York: Kingfisher, 2011.

Curnick, Pippa, and Jen Feroze. *Let's Explore . . . Ocean*. Franklin, Tenn.: Lonely Planet Kids, 2016.

Hughes, Catherine D. *National Geographic: Little Kids' First Big Book of the Ocean*. Washington, DC: National Geographic Children's Books, 2013.

Kainen, Dan, and Carol Kaufmann. *Ocean: A Photicular Book*. New York: Workman Publishing Company, 2014.

Web Sites

Encyclopedia Britannica Kids—Mediterranean Sea
   https://kids.britannica.com/comptons/article-9275768/Mediterranean-Sea

KonnectHQ—Sea Facts
   https://www.konnecthq.com/sea-facts/

GLOSSARY

anemone (uh-NEH-moh-nee)— A round shaped sea animal that has stinging tentacles around its mouth.

baleen (BAL-een)—Large filters that hang down from the upper jaw of baleen whales, such as fin whales.

filter (FIL-ter)—To act like a screen by letting water through and blocking or trapping dirt, food, and other things.

prey (PRAY)—An animal that is hunted for food.

Sicily (SIH-suh-lee)—The largest island in the Mediterranean Sea.

tentacle (TEN-tih-kul)—A flexible limb on an animal.

tropical (TRAH-pih-kul)—From the warm part of the earth that is near the equator.

venom (VEH-num)—A poison produced by certain animals, such as moray eels and stingrays.

PHOTO CREDITS

pp. 4-5—Shutterstock/Goldilock Project; p. 5 (inset)—Shutterstock/Andrew Sutton; p. 7—Heather Paul; pp. 8-9—Shutterstock/Leonardo Gonzalez; p. 9 (inset)—Shutterstock/Brian Clifford; pp. 10-11—Shutterstock/Mark-Anthony Falzon; p. 8 (inset), 22-23—Shutterstock/Alexey Masliy; pp. 12-13—Shutterstock/Alessandro De Maddalena; p. 13 (inset)—Shutterstock/Sergey Novikov; pp. 14-15—Shutterstock/Martin Prochazkacz; pp. 16-17—Shutterstock/Al Carrera; p. 16 (inset)—Shutterstock/boulham; pp. 18-19—Shutterstock/ Allexxandar; p. 19 (inset)—Shutterstock/Jesus Cobaleda; pp. 20-21—Shutterstock/Wirestock Creators; p. 21 (inset)—Shutterstock/LGraz84; p. 23 (inset)—Shutterstock/Gerry Bishop; pp. 24-25—Shutterstock/NaturePicsFilms; p. 24 (inset)—Shutterstock/SLSK Photography; pp. 26-27—Shutterstock/zaferkizilkaya; p. 27 (inset)—Shuterstock/Andrea Izzotti; pp. 28-29—Shutterstock/Matt Gibson; p. 29 (inset)—Shutterstock/Fuciu Catalin. All other photos—Public Domain.

INDEX

Anemones 2
Basking shark 14–15
Blue whale 8
Bottlenose dolphin 6–7
Cuttlefish 22–23
Fin whale 8–9
Ghost crab 20–21
Greater weever 18–19
Jellyfish 10–11
Loggerhead turtle 24–25
Mauve stinger 11
Mediterranean gulls 28–29
Mediterranean monk seals 26–27
Pilot whale 4–5
Sea urchins 16–17, 25
Shortfin mako shark 12–13
Striped dolphin 6
Tidal pools 2
Whitetip shark 12–13

© 2025 by Curious Fox Books™, an imprint of Fox Chapel Publishing Company, Inc.

Magnificent Creatures of the Mediterranean Sea is a revision of *Water Planet: Life in the Mediterranean Sea*, originally published in 2018 by Purple Toad Publishing, Inc. Reproduction of its contents is strictly prohibited without written permission from the rights holder.

Paperback ISBN 979-8-89094-180-0
Hardcover ISBN 979-8-89094-181-7

Library of Congress Control Number: 2024950038

To learn more about the other great books from Fox Chapel Publishing, or to find a retailer near you, call toll-free at 800-457-9112 or visit us at *www.FoxChapelPublishing.com*.
You can also send mail to:
Fox Chapel Publishing
903 Square Street
Mount Joy, PA 17552

We are always looking for talented authors. To submit an idea, please send a brief inquiry to acquisitions@foxchapelpublishing.com.

Fox Chapel Publishing makes every effort to use environmentally friendly paper for printing.

Printed in China